FASCINATI

FOR

YEAR OLD KIDS

WHITE CHOCOLATE
isn't actually chocolate.

The world's largest cup of tea was made in 2010 in Bangladesh and contained over **3 MILLION** cups of tea.

The world's oldest known fruit is the **FIG**, dating back to around 9,000 years ago.

The world's largest pizza ever made was over **2 MILES** long and was made in Rome, Italy in 2012.

Carrots were originally **PURPLE**.

People once thought **TOMATOES** were poisonous.

The world's largest ice cream sundae was made in Edmonton, Canada in 1988 and weighed over **24,000 POUNDS.**

The world's largest hamburger weighed over **2800 POUNDS** and was made in 2012 in Missouri, USA.

HONEY is regurgitated by bees.

Sweet potatoes aren't **YAMS**.

Tootsie Pops can take **HUNDREDS** of licks to get to the center.

The world's largest gummy worm weighs over **3,000 POUNDS.**

FOR 9 YEAR OLDS

French fries aren't actually from **FRANCE.**

The world's largest omelet weighed over **6000 POUNDS** and was made in 2011 in China.

The world's oldest known cookbook is from ancient Mesopotamia and dates back to around **1700 BCE.**

The world's largest pizza delivery was made by Domino's Pizza in 2001, delivering over **11,000** pizzas to troops in Bosnia and Herzegovina.

The world's first chocolate factory was established in Switzerland in **1819.**

Cauliflower comes in **FOUR** colors.

The world's first frozen food was made by the ancient **CHINESE** over 2,000 years ago, who froze fruits and vegetables during the winter months.

Greek yogurt is high in protein but is quite **BAD** for the environment.

The world's largest chocolate sculpture weighed over **10,000** pounds and was made in Italy in 2011.

The world's first food canning factory was established in **1812** by Nicolas Appert in France, who canned food in glass jars.

The avocado is a **FRUIT**, not a **vegetable**.

The world's largest cheesecake weighed over **8,000 POUNDS** and was made in New York in 2010.

The world's hottest chili pepper is the **CAROLINA REAPER,** which can measure up to 2.2 million Scoville heat units.

The highest ever recorded speed for a pitched baseball is **105.1 MPH,** thrown by Aroldis Chapman.

The most successful Olympian of all time is **MICHAEL PHELPS**, with a total of 23 gold medals and 3 silver medals.

The **KENTUCKY DERBY** is the oldest continually held sports event in the United States (1875), with the second being the Westminster Kennel Club Dog show (1876).

The first modern Olympic Games were held in **ATHENS,** Greece in 1896.

The most successful country in Olympic history is the **UNITED STATES.**

Boxing became a legal sport in
1896.

The most successful country in
FIFA World Cup history is BRAZIL,
with a total of 5 championships.

The longest professional baseball game
ever played was **33** innings.

There are over 8000 different sports in the world.

The record for the most career innings in Major League Baseball is held by Cy Young with 7,356.

The first Olympic Games were held in 776 BC in Olympia, Greece and lasted for one day.

The very first Olympic race, held in **776 BC,** was won by Coroebus, a chef.

Rugby balls are made from
LEATHER.

On February 6th, 1971, Alan Shepard hit a golf ball on the **MOON.**

Umpire Joe West has the record for most games served with **5,376**.

The first recorded game of basketball was played in **1892** in Springfield, Massachusetts.

The 1912 Olympics was the last time that gold medals were made of **SOLID GOLD**

The only sport in which left-handed people have a distinct advantage is FENCING.

A baseball has exactly 108 stitches; a cricket ball has between 78 and 82 stitches.

The only Olympic sport in which the contestants are barefoot is TAEKWONDO.

The first recorded game of American football was played in **1869** between Princeton and Rutgers.

The first recorded game of baseball was played in **1846** in Hoboken, New Jersey.

The first recorded game of soccer was played in **CHiNA** in 2nd and 3rd century BC.

The first recorded game of ice hockey was played in Montreal, Canada in 1875.

The first recorded game of golf was played in Scotland in the 15TH CENTURY.

The number pi (π) has been known for almost 4,000 years and was famously calculated to over a million digits by Archimedes of Syracuse.

The symbol for pi (π) was first used by mathematician William Jones in **1706.**

A **CiRCLE** also has the shortest perimeter of any shape with the same area.

The number e, known as **EULER'S** number, is a mathematical constant approximately equal to 2.71828 and is used in many areas of mathematics, including calculus and number theory.

 **"FOUR"** is the only number, when written in English, whose spelling contains the same number of letters as the number itself.

The number zero (**0**) was invented by the ancient Indians and was passed on to the Arabic world where it was further developed and spread to Europe.

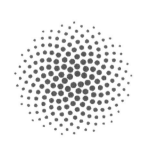 The **FiBONACCi** sequence is a series of numbers in which each number is the sum of the two preceding ones, usually starting with 0 and 1.

A 'jiffy' is an actual unit of time. It means **1/100** th of a second.

Have you ever noticed that the opposite sides of a die always add up to seven (**7**).

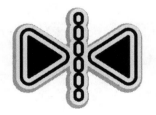 A **PALINDROME** number is one that reads the same backwards and forward, e.g. 1331.

FOR 9 YEAR OLDS

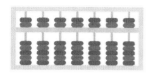 **ABACUS** is considered the origin of the calculator.

An **ICOSAGON** is a shape with 20 sides.

 **TRiGONOMETRY** is the study of the relationship between the angles of triangles and their sides.

 A hexagon is a shape with **6** sides.

What comes after a million, billion, and trillion? A **QUADRiLLiON**.

1,000,000,000,000 ,000

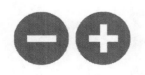 Plus (+) and Minus (−) sign symbols were used as early as **1557 A.D.**

FOR 9 YEAR OLDS

 2520 is the first number to be divisible by all numbers from **1-10.**

If you multiply 21978 by 4, it **REVERSES** : 87912.

 **FORTY** is the only number that is spelt with the numbers arranged in alphabetical order.

The word "hundred" comes from an ancient Norse term, **"HUNDRATH"**. Funny thing is that hundrath means 120, not 100.

The number 5040 has exactly **60** divisors.

The **GOLDEN RATIO** (phi) is a mathematical concept found in many natural and man-made structures, including the Great Pyramid of Giza, the Parthenon, and the Mona Lisa.

FOR 9 YEAR OLDS

The Sun makes a full rotation once every **27** days.

Earth is the only planet **NOT** named after a god.

Pluto is **SMALLER** than the United States in terms of area.

Your skin has **1000** different species of bacteria on it.

Your strongest and longest bone is your **FEMUR**.

The human brain has a memory capacity which is estimated to be about **2.5 PETABYTES.**

Your skull is made up of **8** different bones.

Nerve impulses sent from the brain move at a speed of **432 KM/H.**

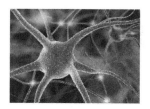

The human embryo acquires fingerprints within **6 MONTHS** of conception.

The average person forgets **90%** of their dreams.

The total length of all the blood vessels in the human body is about **100,000** miles.

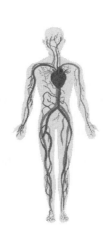

We lose 10% of our body heat from the **HEAD.**

 Humans are the only animals that shed **TEARS** when they are sad or happy.

Humans are the only animals that can recognize themselves in a **MIRROR.**

 Not only human beings, **KOALAS** also have unique fingerprints.

Only **1%** of the bacteria can result in the human body becoming ill.

The scientific name for the belly button is the **UMBiLiCUS.**

TEETH are the only part of the human body which cannot heal themselves.

On average, a person needs
20 MINUTES to fall asleep.

Over **37 TRILLION** cells

make up the human body.

Only about **11%** of people are

left-handed.

The average human heart beats about **100,000** times per day.

There are more than **200** different viruses which can cause a cold.

Women blink about **TWO** times more often than men.

 **HUMANS** have the largest brain size in proportion to body size of any animal species.

100,000 chemical reactions occur in the human brain **EVERY SECOND.**

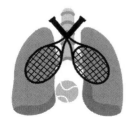 The surface area of the human lungs is approximately equal to the area of a **TENNIS** court.

Humans are the only animals that can experience religious and spiritual BELiEFS.

The ancient Egyptians used a hieroglyphic script made up of over 700 symbols.

In ancient Rome, GLADiATORiAL contests were considered to be the highest form of entertainment.

The **MAGNA CARTA**, signed in 1215, is considered to be one of the most important legal documents in history as it helped to establish the principle of the rule of law.

Pope Gregory IV declared a war on CATS.

The ancient MAYANS were skilled astronomers and were able to predict solar eclipses with great accuracy.

The Great Wall of China is the longest wall in the world, stretching over 13,000 miles.

The ancient Greeks believed that the world was made up of **FOUR** elements: earth, air, fire, and water.

The SIKH religion was founded by Guru Nanak in the 15th century in the Punjab region of India and Pakistan.

FOR 9 YEAR OLDS

TURKEYS were once worshiped as gods. The Mayan people believed turkeys were the vessels of the gods and honored them with worship.

The GOLDEN TEMPLE, also known as Harmandir Sahib, is the most important pilgrimage site for Sikhs and is located in the city of Amritsar, Punjab.

During World War I, the French built a "FAKE PARiS". It was built as a means of throwing off German bomber and fighter pilots flying over French skies.

FOR 9 YEAR OLDS

The ancient Egyptians believed that the **PHARAOHS** were divine and that they were responsible for maintaining order in the world.

Thomas Edison **DIDN'T** actually invent many of the things he patented.

The **BLACK DEATH**, a devastating plague that swept through Europe in the 14th century, is believed to have killed over 25 million people.

The **BRiTiSH** Empire was the largest empire in the world at its height.

The ancient **CHiNESE** invented gunpowder, paper money, and the printing press.

The ancient Incas of South America had a complex road system that spanned over **25,000** miles.

It's believed that roughly **97%** of history has been lost over time. Written accounts of history only started roughly 6,000 years ago. And modern humans first appeared around 200,000 years ago.

Christianity is based on the life, teachings, and death of JESUS CHRIST, who is considered the Son of God by its followers.

Christianity originated in the Middle East in the **1ST CENTURY** AD and spread throughout the Roman Empire.

CHRISTIANITY has many denominations, including Roman Catholicism, Eastern Orthodoxy, and Protestantism.

Maharaja **RANJIT SINGH** was the founder of the Sikh Empire, which lasted from 1799 to 1849.

The holy book of Sikhism is the **GURU GRANTH SAHIB**, which contains the teachings of the religion's 10 Gurus.

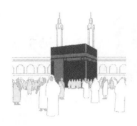

ISLAM is the second largest religion in the world, with over 1.8 billion followers.

The central text of Islam is the **QURAN**, believed by Muslims to be the literal word of God as revealed to the prophet Muhammad.

MARS has lower gravity than Earth.

If you add up opposite sides of a die, you will always get **7**.

The word "fraction" comes from the Latin word fractio, which means **"TO BREAK"**.

The concept of **INFINITY** was first introduced by the ancient Greek mathematician Zeno of Elea.

Uranus' blue glow is due to the **GASES** in its atmosphere.

Pluto's largest moon, Charon, is **HALF** the size of Pluto.

Neptune takes nearly **165** Earth years to make one orbit of the Sun.

The **MARTIAN DAY** is 24 hours 39 minutes and 35 seconds long.

A day on Pluto lasts for
153.3 HOURS.

The **INTERNATIONAL SPACE STATION** is the largest manned object ever sent into space.

The largest known star is UY Scuti, which is around **1,700** times larger than the sun.

The **MARiNER 10** was the first spacecraft that visited Mercury in 1974.

The closest star to Earth is **PROXiMA CENTAURi**, located 4.22 light years away.

 The Milky Way galaxy is estimated to contain around **100 BILLION** planets.

The largest known galaxy is IC 1101, which is estimated to be around **6 MILLION** light years across.

 The largest known black hole is located in the galaxy NGC 1277, and is estimated to be **17 BILLION** times the mass of the Sun.

The International Space Station circles Earth every
90 MINUTES.

The first human-made object to leave our solar system is the Voyager 1 probe, which was launched in 1977.

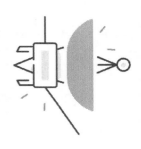

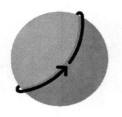

The Earth's rotation is
SLOWING slightly as time goes on.

 Light travels from the Sun to the Earth in less than **10 MiNUTES**.

The temperature of deep space is around **2.7** Kelvin (–270.45 Celsius or –454.81 Fahrenheit)

 The first artificial satellite in space was called **"SPUTNiK"**.

The closest planet to Earth is
VENUS.

Jupiter is the **LARGEST** planet in our solar system.

The first woman in space was
VALENTINA TERESHKOVA,
who flew on the Vostok 6
mission in 1963.

In Western culture, **WHITE** often represents innocence, peace, and purity, and is often used in weddings. However, in China, white is associated with death and mourning and often worn to funerals.

Different colors evoke different EMOTIONS.

The most common color for highlighters is YELLOW because it doesn't leave a shadow on the page when photocopied.

Zuckerberg happens to be **RED-GREEN** colorblind, which is why he chose blue as the main color for the Facebook logo.

The first Coca Cola logo was colored in **BLACK**.

GREEN is associated with health and prosperity.

 The Sun is actually **WHiTE**. When viewed from space or a high altitude, it appears in its true color of white. When viewed from a low altitude, the atmosphere makes it look yellow.

Yellow is known to stimulate **HUNGER**.

 Grey is considered a **NEUTRAL** color.

BLACK radiates elegance and power in some cultures.

The color of an object is **NOT** actually the color of the object itself, but rather the color of the light that the object reflects or emits. For example, a red apple is not actually red; it absorbs all colors of light except red, which it reflects, making it appear red to our eyes.

CHROMOPHOBIA is the fear of colors.

Humans can see more shades of green than any other color, due to the high number of receptors in the eye that are sensitive to **GREEN** light.

The color **RED** is often used as a warning or danger signal, as it is the color that is most easily seen from a distance.

Many animals see a **DIFFERENT** range of colors than humans do. For example, some birds and insects can see ultraviolet light, while many animals, such as dogs and cats, have fewer color receptors in their eyes than humans and can only see a limited range of colors.

Cheddar cheese is only orange because it is DYED.

In ancient Egypt, BLUE was considered to be a sacred color and was associated with the gods and the pharaohs. The ancient Egyptians developed a pigment called Egyptian blue, which was used in art and architecture.

In many cultures, the color GOLD is associated with wealth, luxury, and prestige.

The color **BROWN** is often associated with nature and earthy tones since it is a warm and neutral color. It can also be associated with stability and reliability.

Lake **HILLIER** is a bubble-gum-pink lake right on the edge of Recherché Archipelago's largest island in Australia.

YELLOW is considered a royal color in Chinese culture. Historically, only the emperor was allowed to wear yellow clothing, and it was seen as a symbol of power and authority. Yellow is also associated with wealth and prosperity, and is often used in traditional Chinese architecture and decoration.

In the Middle Ages, **PURPLE** dye was extremely rare and costly to produce, as it was made from a type of sea snail called a "purpura." Due to its expense, it was often associated with wealth and luxury and was worn by royalty and the elite.

The color **ORANGE** is known to be associated with energy, warmth and enthusiasm. It is also believed to stimulate mental activity, appetite and is often used to promote food products.

Some shark species lay **EGGS** instead of living pups.

FOR 9 YEAR OLDS

The color PiNK is often associated with femininity and is sometimes considered a "girly" color. However, it wasn't always that way, the association of the color pink with femininity is a relatively recent development, and it was traditionally considered a masculine color.

Though experienced, **WHALES** can lose their way during migration.

CAMELS are a good source of milk, wool, and meat and are used for transportation or carrying heavy loads as well.

The color **SiLVER** is often associated with elegance, sophistication, and modernity. It can also be associated with the moon and the night sky, and it is used in a variety of products such as mirrors, jewelry, and silverware.

Creatures like sea **LiCE** and barnacles stick to the whale's skin and live there all their lives.

LiONS do not possess a lot of stamina, meaning they can run only in short bursts.

FOR 9 YEAR OLDS

A male giraffe fights using its **NECK** by swinging it from one side to the other.

Male elephants leave their herds when they reach **13** years of age, while females live in their herd for their entire lifetime.

A full-grown male giraffe can weigh up to **1400** kilograms.

 Cheetahs are the only members of the cat family unable to **ROAR**.

Honeybees can flap their wings up to 200 times per second.

 A group of owls is called a **PARLiAMENT.**

There are **32** muscles in a cat's ear.

BATS are the only mammals that have the ability to fly.

 Dolphins give **NAMES** to each other.

Gorillas can catch human **COLDS** .

Goats can have **ACCENTS**.

A **BAT** can eat up to 1 thousand insects per hour.

FOR 9 YEAR OLDS

 Octopuses have **THREE** hearts.

A group of skunks is called a
STENCH.

 A **STARFISH** can turn its stomach inside out.

A group of porcupines is called a
PRiCKLE.

The platypus is one of only a few mammals that lays **EGGS** instead of giving birth to live young.

A crab's taste buds are on their **FEET**.

A woodpecker's tongue actually wraps all the way around its **BRAIN**, protecting it from damage when it's hammering into a tree.

The first spam email was sent in **1978** by a computer seller.

The **CHAMELEON** can rotate its eyes independently, allowing it to keep watch for predators and prey at the same time.

The first ever internet message was sent by computer engineer Charles K. Kline in 1969, which read **"LO".**

The introduction of MP3 changed music in **1995.**

The first emoticon was created in **1982** by computer scientist Scott Fahlman.

FOR 9 YEAR OLDS

Twitter was originally called
TWTTR.

The first YouTube video was uploaded in **2005**.

Around **7 MILLION** blog posts get published per day.

The first webpage is still
ONLiNE.

The internet is more than **11,500** days old.

The average growth rate of internet users is **4.8%** per year.

FOR 9 YEAR OLDS

Asia has the largest number of internet users at just about 2 billion.

32% of Internet users worldwide are 25 TO 34 years old.

The Chrome web browser is used by about 65% of internet users worldwide.

87% of internet users use the
GOOGLE search engine.

Google Search Index contains more
than **100,000,000** GB.

YouTube has over **2 BILLION**
active users.

Twitter has over **400 MiLLiON** unique users.

FiNLAND is the first country in the world to make internet access a legal right.

Reddit has over **430 MiLLiON** active monthly users.

Over **5 TRiLLiON** dollars in estimated sales of products and services occured via the Internet in 2021.

Hackers attack every **39** seconds across the world.

The first ever online purchase was made in **1994** by a man named Phil Brandenberger, who bought a Sting album on AOL.

FOR 9 YEAR OLDS

The first ever online message board was created in **1979** by a computer science professor at the University of Delaware.

There were over **367 MiLLiON** domain names registered in 2021.

It is possible to get internet service and cell reception on **MT. EVEREST.**

Lettuce is a member of the **DAiSY** family.

ASiA is the largest continent in the world.

The best place to see rainbows is **HAWAii** because they are the brightest there.

The **GREAT BARRiER REEF,** located off the coast of Australia, is the largest living structure on Earth, and is visible from space. It is made up of thousands of individual coral reefs and is home to a wide variety of marine life, including over 1,500 species of fish and 400 species of coral. It is also the largest coral reef system in the world.

SAiNT LUCiA is the only country in the world named after a woman.

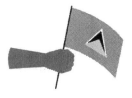

There is a town in Nebraska called Monowi with a population of **ONE.**

The world's deepest postbox is located in Susami Bay in Japan, at a depth of **10 METERS** (33 feet) underwater. It was installed in 2002 to provide divers with an opportunity to send postcards while they were diving.

Mercury and Venus are the only two planets in our solar system that do not have any **MOONS**.

According to the Centers for Disease Control and Prevention (CDC), the average number of deaths on cruise ships per year is around **20**.

The world's tallest waterfall is **ANGEL FALLS** in Venezuela, which has a height of 979 meters (3,212 feet) from the top of the cliff to the bottom of the pool. The waterfall is not easily accessible though since it is located in a remote jungle. It can only be reached by boat or by hiking through the jungle.

The unique smell of **RAIN** actually comes from plant oils, bacteria, and ozone.

The tallest tree in the world is a coast redwood named **HYPERION**. It stands at 379.7 feet (115.7 meters) tall.

The world's largest volcano is **MAUNA LOA** on the island of Hawaii. It is a shield volcano, which means it has gentle slopes. It is about 4,169 meters (13,678 feet) tall and its base covers an area of about 5,271 square kilometers (2,033 square miles). Mauna Loa is also an active volcano, and it last erupted in 1984.

If you **HEAT** up a magnet, it will lose its magnetism.

The deepest point in the ocean is the Challenger Deep, located in the Mariana Trench in the Pacific Ocean. It is about **36,070** feet (10,994 meters) deep.

The world's largest desert is the **ANTARCTIC** Desert. While it may not have the same kind of sand dunes as other deserts, it is still considered a desert due to its low precipitation. The Antarctic desert is about 14 million square kilometers (5.4 million square miles) and is covered by ice and snow.

The largest mammal migration on Earth is the **WILDBEEST** migration in Tanzania and Kenya, where over 1.5 million wildbeest and 200,000 zebras travel annually in search of fresh grazing.

DENTISTRY is one of the oldest professions in the world.

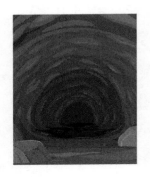

The largest cave in the world is the cave **HANG SON DOONG** in Vietnam, which is over 5.5 miles long, 650 feet high and 490 feet wide. It was discovered in 1991 by a local man named Ho Khanh but wasn't explored by scientists until 2009. The cave is so large that it has its own climate and even has a jungle inside.

Without a **TONGUE**, humans are unable to taste food.

The highest point on Earth is Mount Everest, located in the Himalayas on the border of Nepal and Tibet. It stands at **29,029** feet (8,848 meters) tall.

The longest river in the world is the **NILE**, stretching 4,132 miles (6,650 kilometers) through 11 countries in Africa, including Egypt, Sudan, and Ethiopia. It is the primary water source for many communities and is a significant source of irrigation and hydroelectric power

Times Square was originally called Long Acre Square until it was renamed in **1904** after The New York Times moved its headquarters to the newly built Times Building.

The longest living mammal is the bowhead whale, which can live up to **200** years.

The largest living organism on Earth is a **FUNGUS** called Armillaria ostoyae, also known as the "honey mushroom." It covers 2,200 acres (890 hectares) of land in Oregon, USA, and it is estimated to be around 2,400 years old.

The largest statue in the world is the Spring Temple **BUDDHA** in China, standing at a height of 153 meters (502 feet). It is made of copper and steel, and it was completed in 2008.

The largest animal to ever live is the blue whale, which can grow up to 100 feet long and weigh as much as **200** tons.

The largest lake in the world by area is the CASPiAN Sea, located between Europe and Asia. It has an area of 371,000 square kilometers (143,000 square miles) and is not considered a sea because it lacks a connection to the ocean.

The GREAT WALL OF CHiNA is the only man-made structure visible from space with the naked eye.

The smallest mammal in the world is the bumblebee bat, which is only 29–33 millimeters (1.14–1.3 inches) long and weighs less than a PENNY.

FOR 9 YEAR OLDS

The animal with the most legs is the millipede, which can have up to **750** legs.

The Mona Lisa has no **EYEBROWS** because they were removed during the conservation process.

The world's oldest city is Jericho, located in the Palestine territories, which dates back to **8000 BC.**

The world's largest ocean is the **PACiFiC** Ocean, covering about 60 million square miles.

The world's largest canyon is the Grand Canyon in Arizona, measuring over **277** miles long, 18 miles wide and over a mile deep.

Astronauts get slightly **TALLER** when in space.

The world's largest pyramid is the Great Pyramid of Giza in Egypt, measuring over **480** feet tall.

The **EiFFEL TOWER** was originally intended as a temporary structure and was almost dismantled in 1909.

There are more **STARS** in space than there are grains of sand on every beach in the world.

Kangaroos keep growing until they DiE.

A snail can sleep for
3 YEARS.

In California, you can get a ticket if you're driving
TOO SLOWLY.

The tallest mountain in the solar system is Olympus Mons, located on

MARS.

The fear of vegetables is called
LACHANOPHOBIA.

The collective name for a group of unicorns is called a **BLESSING.**

The world's oldest known sample of DNA is over **1 MILLION** years old and was found in a fossilized insect encased in amber.

A sneeze travels at **100** miles per hour.

The world's tallest mammal is the **GIRAFFE**, which can grow up to 18 feet tall.

The world's tallest roller coaster, Kingda Ka, is located at Six Flags Great Adventure in New Jersey, USA, and reaches a height of **456 FEET** (139 m).

You cannot sneeze with your **EYES OPEN.**

DUBAI has no personal income tax.

 Black blizzards occur when DiRT mixes with the wind.

Heavy snowfall can completely diminish ViSiBiLiTY.

 Some tornadoes can be faster than FORMULA ONE racing cars.

The **"FiRE RAiNBOWS"** or "circumhorizontal arcs" are a rare meteorological phenomenon caused by the refraction of light through ice crystals in the atmosphere, resulting in a rainbow-colored band that appears parallel to the horizon.

Human activity affects the
WEATHER.

TUNDRA zones are the coldest climates.

"HALO STORMS" are a rare weather phenomenon where a ring of light appears around the sun or moon, caused by the refraction of light through ice crystals in the atmosphere.

High altitudes are **COOLER** than lower altitudes.

"GREEN FLASH" is a rare meteorological phenomenon that can be observed at sunset or sunrise, when a green flash of light appears above the sun for a moment.

Nearly **2,000** thunderstorms are happening over the planet at any given time.

Lightning typically follows a
VOLCANIC ERUPTION

Cats and dogs are able to sense when a **TORNADO** is approaching.

The strongest ever recorded wind was on Mt Washington, New Hampshire, USA at an amazing

231 MPH.

The coldest temperature ever recorded was **-89.2°C** (–128.6°F).

In 1899, the Mississippi River became completely frozen because it was so **COLD**.

The lowest temperature recorded was on July 21, 1983, in **VOSTOK,** Antarctica.

The sunniest place on earth is **ARIZONA.**

The. **ATMOSPHERE** is made of 78% Nitrogen, 21% Oxygen, 0.9% Argon, 0.03% Carbon Dioxide.

 **METEOROLOGY** is the study of weather patterns and the atmosphere.

During flashes of lightning, it is advisable to stay indoors as it is very **RiSKY** and can cause death. Also be sure to avoid trees if you are outside!

 The hottest temperature recorded was in **GREENLAND RANCH** in Death Valley, California on July 10, 1913.

The driest place on earth is
ATACAMA.

The wettest place on earth
is **MAWSYNRAM**,
Meghalaya, India.

THUNDER is caused by
lightning.

FOR 9 YEAR OLDS

Leave Your Feedback on Amazon

Please think about leaving some feedback via a review on Amazon. It may only take a moment, but it really does mean the world for small businesses like mine.

Even if you did not enjoy this title, please let us know the reason(s) in your review so that we may improve this title and serve you better.

From the Publisher

Hayden Fox's mission is to create premium content for children that will help them expand their vocabulary, grow their imaginations, gain confidence, and share tons of laughs along the way.

Without you, however, this would not be possible, so we sincerely thank you for your purchase and for supporting our company mission.

Don't forget your free gifts!

(My way of saying thank you for your support)

Simply visit **haydenfoxmedia.com** to receive the following:

- 10 Powerful Dinner Conversations To Create Amazing Kids

- 10 Magical Affirmations To Help Kids Become Unstoppable in Life

(you can also scan this QR code)

More titles you're sure to love!

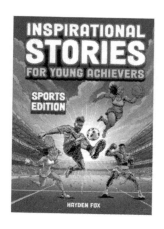

HAYDEN FOX

Made in the USA
Las Vegas, NV
31 October 2023